Toolkit #2

The Top Twenty Sustainability Strategies for Nonprofits

Techniques to ensure long-term stability and growth

Marilyn L. Donnellan, MS

The Top Twenty Sustainability Strategies for Nonprofits

One of the Nonprofit **Toolkit** series
Nonprofit Toolkits:
Tool #1: Volunteer Handbooks
Tool #2: The Top Twenty Sustainability Strategies for Nonprofits
Tool #3: Becoming a Tech-Focused Nonprofit

Published by CreateSpace
©2018, by Marilyn L. Donnellan, Author

All rights reserved. This includes the right to reproduce any portion of this book in any form. The author and publisher specifically disclaim any responsibility for any liability, loss, or risk, personal or otherwise, incurred as a consequence, directly or indirectly, of the use and application of any of the contents of this book. Although every precaution has been taken in the preparation of this book, the publisher and authors assume no responsibility for errors or omissions.

ISBN – 13: 978-1985882171
ISBN – 10: 1985882175

Table of Contents	Page
Chapter One: Importance of Building Sustainability Strategies	5
Chapter Two: Building Sustainability Strategies Throughout the Organization	11
Chapter Three: Establishing Sustainable Programs	26
Chapter Four: Implementing a Sustainable Resource Development Program	33
Chapter Five: Developing Administrative Strategies to Support Sustainability	42
Chapter Six: Developing Sustainable Board and Volunteer Development Programs	53
Chapter Seven: Implementing Sustainable Marketing Strategies	70
Chapter Eight: Expanding Community Involvement	76

All material, figures and addendums are copyrighted and based on the books in the Nonprofit Management Simplified series, ©2017 CharityChannel Press,
M. L. Donnellan, MS, Author

Figures	Page
1: Sustainability Strategies Chart	10
2: Core Elements Chart	12
3: Core Elements Rating Chart	16
4: Steps for Implementing Outcomes Measurements	29
5: Fundraising as Percentage of Total Income	36
6: Fundraising Costs	40
7: Executive Director Succession Plan	44
8: Virtual Volunteer Examples	58
9: Board, Staff Roles & Responsibilities	65
10: Community Problem-Solving Silos	87
Addendums	**Page**
A: Policies and Procedures Manual Checklist	88
B: Sample Simplified Strategic Plan	93
C: Sample Committee Chair and Vice Chair Job Descriptions	94
D: Sample Officer Job Descriptions	99
E: Simplified Parliamentary Procedures	103
F: Sustainability Assessment	105
About the Author	107
Other Books by Donnellan	107
Connect with the Author	108

Chapter One

Importance of Sustainability Strategies

A few years ago, I received a very sad email from a colleague. Although we had not met in person, we often corresponded via email, sharing both the joys and woes of nonprofit management. In this email, she told me that the organization she started several years earlier was dying. She was heartbroken.

I gently asked her if she would be willing to share more details on what happened. Maybe it was because I was a neutral party, or because I was not a part of her local community, but she opened her heart to me and candidly talked about why she thought this nonprofit, and whose mission was so important to the community, had failed.

The lessons she learned are, unfortunately, symptomatic of very common sustainability strategies often ignored in the exciting start-up phase of an organization. I've included her lessons in the strategies in this guide. But it is not just start-up nonprofits that can ignore these strategies.

I worked with a nonprofit which had served their community for more than 50 years. But when their long-time executive director (ED) left, the interim ED discovered a mess. The financial system was in such disarray that the small organization had to fork over more than $100,000 in auditor fees to just figure out what their financial condition was. The donor database had not been updated in years, so there were no records of previous years' donor contributions and no way of knowing who had contributed what.

When I talked to corporate leaders in the community about the nonprofit it was clear it had a very negative reputation. The board was uninvolved and had no idea what was going on. In one fell swoop, three of the five staff left and now there was little to no institutional memory left. And that didn't even begin to address the problems of outdated and lackluster programs with no measurable outcomes.

In both instances, the start-up nonprofit and the established nonprofit were in big trouble not because their missions and programs were not needed, but because somewhere along the line they failed to include sustainability strategies into their basic daily functions. So, what are the critical sustainability strategies you can incorporate into your organization so your nonprofit does not go belly up, failing your clients and your community?

First, let's define "sustainability." It is often used in an environmental context, as in "sustainable environment," and refers to adequate and renewable clean water and pollution-free air. The term can also be used to convey the concept of supporting, renewing, upholding or confirming in the pursuit of a common ideal. In for-profit business, sustainability usually has both backward-looking measurements and forward-looking indicators. In the nonprofit sector, this has become known as "outcomes measurements." In other words, donors want to know, "Because I gave my money to you, what differences did it make in the community?" If you cannot show the donor what those differences (outcomes) are, chances are your mission will not be sustainable in the long-run.

Secondly, sustainability is not just about funding. Too often I hear nonprofit executives say, "if only we had more money," as though money will solve all their problems. Believe me, money alone will not guarantee sustainability.

A small church in our community received almost $10 million after a parishioner won the lottery. Fantastic, right? They built a state-of-the-art facility: two swimming pools, a large worship center, a youth center, basketball court, etc. Initially, the church membership numbers exploded. But within ten years the church went bankrupt. Why?

Because they had no sustainability strategies. There was no plan to pay for the daily upkeep costs of the huge facility and the inexperienced staff had no clue how to cope with the influx of membership.

Sustainability is not just about survival or keeping the doors open. True sustainability is about building a solid infrastructure, and a culture of innovation, creativity and growth. It means building programs which can be replicated in other communities. Sustainability goes beyond achieving your mission to expanding your mission to better meet the changing needs within your community.

So, what are some key strategies to help you and your nonprofit build sustainability to insure your future success? In this guide, I will take you through what are the proven top twenty strategies anyone can use to build sustainability within the culture of your nonprofit, as shown in Fig. 1. Each of the chapters will deal with the strategies as they relate to the categories shown in the chart.

Look carefully at each of these strategies to see which ones you are already implementing and which ones you are not. At the end of the guide will be an assessment tool (Addendum F) to help you evaluate where you are in implementation of each strategy.

Use the assessment results, along with the assessment tools in the Nonprofit Management Simplified books to build long-term sustainability in your nonprofit.

By the way, start right now to change your thinking from a magic-bullet, short-term approach to sustainability, to a long-term, methodical implementation of these field-tested strategies.

Fig. 1 – Sustainability Strategies

The Top Twenty Strategies for Building Sustainability

#1 — Balance the Core Elements in the Infrastructure
#2 — Establish Clear & Transformative Vision & Mission
#3 — Embed Metrics Across the Organization
#4 — Implement a Never-ending Strategic Planning Process

Programs	Resource Development	Administration	Board & Volunteer Development	Marketing	Community Involvement
#5 Establish Outcomes Measurements	#7 Diversify Funding Sources	#9 Implement a Senior Staff Succession Plan	#13 Implement a Key Volunteer Succession Plan	#16 Integrate Marketing Throughout the Nonprofit	#18 Build Competitive Advantage
#6 Build Relevant Programs	#8 Evaluate Fundraising Costs vs. Income	#10 Establish Institutional Memory Procedures	#14 Establish Regular Board Training	#17 Demonstrate Value to the Community	#19 Leverage Assets thru Collaboration
		#11 Implement Accelerating Technologies	#15 Recruit High-capacity Volunteers		#20 Establish Leadership Role in the Primary Mission
		#12 Outsource			

Chapter Two

Build Sustainability into the Infrastructure

As you can see in Fig. 1, the arrow at the top highlights four sustainability strategies that must encompass the entire organization. These four strategies deal with the overall basic infrastructure of the nonprofit. If they are not incorporated into your nonprofit, sustainability will eventually become an issue.

Strategy #1: Balance the Core Elements within the Infrastructure

Over the past 35 years I have been extremely fortunate to work with hundreds of nonprofit organizations of all types and sizes, both as an executive director (ED), chief executive officer (CEO), and as a consultant. What I have discovered is a very common problem: lack of solid infrastructure across the organization.

Nonprofits naturally focus most their attention and effort on programs and fundraising (resource development). It makes sense because programs are what the mission of the organization is all about and fundraising is how they pay for it.

However, to run programs and raise money without providing a balanced approach to the other four elements is kind of like trying to build a new house and spending all the money on decorations and furniture but ignoring the construction, plumbing and wiring. A house that doesn't have a solid infrastructure is going to collapse when the first strong wind hits it.

Fig. 2: Core Elements of a Successful Nonprofit

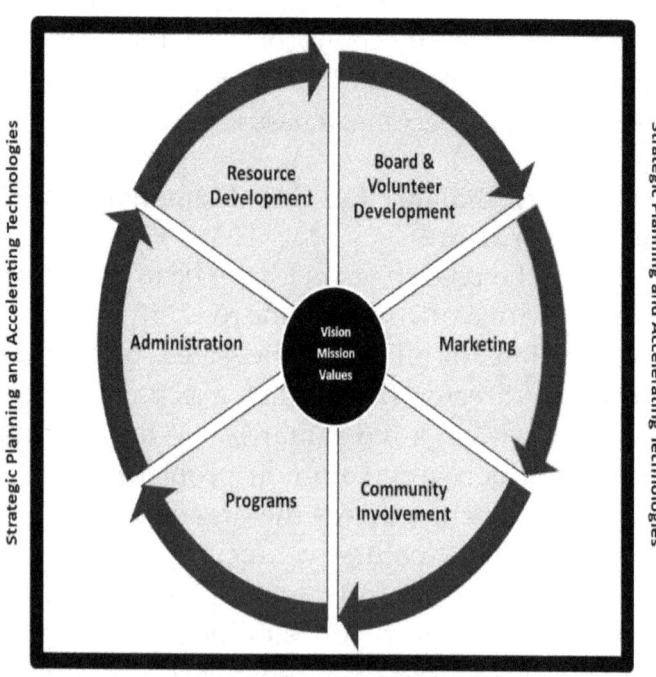

Strategic Planning and Accelerating Technologies

In the same way, a nonprofit that doesn't have a strong infrastructure in all six of the core elements will not be sustainable, especially when times are tough. An overview of these core elements in Fig. 2, leads to the first and maybe the most important and foundational sustainability strategy: balancing your approach to all the core elements within the infrastructure.

When I accepted the position of ED in my first nonprofit, I was the only staff person. I remember one day feeling absolutely overwhelmed at the huge array of tasks in front of me. How could I possibly do everything needing to be done? That was when I began to solidify the concept of the "Core Elements." As I worked to narrow the focus of my job into its basic components, these six categories or core elements bubbled to the top of my thinking:

1. Administration – facilities, finances, equipment, legal issues (like risk management), human resources management

2. Board & volunteer development – recruitment, orientation and training, recognition and dismissal of all three types of volunteers (board, committee and program)

3. Marketing – publicity and all matters related to building brand identity

4. Programs – outcomes measurements and all aspects of program development, evaluation and implementation

5. Community involvement – the wider role the nonprofit plays within the community

6. Resource development – every aspect of raising resources, such as fundraising, planned-giving, gifts in kind, etc.

I had to figure out a way to segment my time across all six of these elements. I also realized the six core elements had to be based on a never-ending strategic planning process, which I will discuss in greater detail as the fourth infrastructure strategy. It is only when those core elements are coordinated and examined regularly through a constantly changing and updated strategic planning process that the nonprofit can build sustainability. And, don't forget to incorporate an accelerating technologies approach, which will be discussed in strategy #11.

To jump start thinking on the core elements, fill in the simple rating chart in Fig. 3. On a scale of 1-5, rate your nonprofit in each of the core elements, with "5" being "excellent."

The purpose of this easy exercise is to help you focus your attention on the importance of being balanced in how you approach ALL aspects of the nonprofit. Have your staff and board members do the rating as well.

Compile the results and then report the results to the board. Even a simple rating exercise like this can help your board begin to think strategically. Included in the strategic planning process in the book, *Nonprofit Management Simplified: Board and Volunteer Development,* is a much more detailed Core Elements Assessment.

If your ratings total 30-35, your nonprofit is in great shape. Your approach to all six of the core elements is probably pretty balanced. A score of 20-29 is good, 10-19 is fair, but anything below 20 may be an indication the organization may not be sustainable in the long run. As you might expect, most nonprofits score 4 or 5 in programs, but generally 2 or less on each of the other five core elements, and especially when rating whether or not they have a never-ending strategic planning process. In evaluating your nonprofit with any type of an assessment, it is really about striving to achieve balance in how you implement all of the six core elements. In other words, make sure you are not spending so much of your time and effort on programs and fundraising that you ignore the other four critical elements.

If your nonprofit is anything less than a "4" in any of the elements, sustainability might become an issue for you in the future.

Fig. 3: Core Elements Rating

Core Elements Rating Chart

Core Element	Rating 1-5 "5"=excellent
Administration	
Board & Volunteer Development	
Marketing	
Community Involvement	
Programs	
Resource Development	
Strategic Planning	
Total	

Now that you have done a simple assessment of all the core elements within your organization, let's look at the heart of your nonprofit: your vision and mission.

Strategy #2: Establish a Clear and Transformative Vision and Mission

Without a clear and transformative vision and mission, sustainability will be a problem. Most nonprofits have vision and mission statements, but when was the last time you and your board looked at them? Are they still valid? Have the programs in the organization changed over the years so that the old vision and mission are no longer relevant? Or has the community changed so much that your vision and mission need to change? Are the statements too long for staff and volunteers to easily remember?

There is an ancient proverb which says, "Where there is no vision the people perish." (Proverbs 29:18). In other words, without a transformative, understandable vision on why the organization exists, it will not be sustainable in the long run. Often nonprofits focus on the mission, but the vision must be what drives the mission. The vision states why the organization serves the community while the mission states what the nonprofit does to achieve the vision. You must have a strong vision (why) before you can establish the mission (how).

For example, a child abuse prevention nonprofit might have as a vision: "All children safe from abuse," while the mission might be, "To educate, protect and serve the victims and families of child abuse."

Notice how succinct both statements are. The mission is the action while the vision is the ultimate dream to achieve. Anyone can remember them when they are short and succinct. The strategic planning process mentioned earlier includes a step by step strategy to review your vision and mission statements which involves the board and senior staff but avoids wordsmithing. Wordsmithing is when too much time is spent agonizing over the wording instead of focusing on the overall meaning.

When I first started facilitating strategic planning sessions, I worked with a nonprofit whose mission statement was two, single-spaced pages long. At the beginning of the session, I asked the group to tell me the vision or the mission of the nonprofit in one sentence. No one could do it. But when the facilitated process was completed, they could narrow their vision and mission statements down to less than 25 words.

So, be sure you have clear, simple vision and mission statements. When you do, the statements can become transformative tools for the marketing strategies. They can become the heart and soul of your organization, transforming staff, volunteers and donors into passionate advocates for what you do.

Strategy #3: Embed Metrics across the Organization

A lot of nonprofit staff and volunteers start groaning when I begin to talk about metrics or numbers. Maybe you weren't good in math in school, so the thought of having to apply statistical analysis to what you do can be not only scary but an incredibly boring idea. You understand counting dollars in your resource development efforts or accounting, but the rest of the organization? Probably not so much.

Let's approach it from a different, practical perspective. Suppose you could see numbers as ways to demonstrate success, a symbolic tool of your achievements, a strategy for embracing essential change, or a way to build sustainability into the nonprofit?

Change is hard for any organization. "But we've always done it this way" might be the seven last words of your nonprofit if you are not willing to see metrics as assessment and evaluation strategies to assure your mission will continue indefinitely to serve the community. Peter Drucker, well known for his books on nonprofit governance said it best, "If leaders are unable to slough off yesterday, to abandon yesterday, they simply will not be able to create tomorrow."

Here are several reasons why metrics are important:

1. Metrics show donors how their contributions are being used, donor

retention rates and their levels of giving (resource development),

2. Metrics show the board you are accountable with financial management, risk management, facilities use, human resources, and meeting legal requirements (administration),

3. Metrics are an encouragement to volunteers to be involved (board and volunteer development)

4. Metrics can be indicators to keep you from heading the wrong direction in your programs (programs),

5. Metrics can determine if your marketing strategies are working (marketing),

6. Metrics demonstrate to the community the impact you are having on a specific issue (community involvement)

7. Metrics show you if you are spending too much time on one core element at the expense of another, or if you are allowing enough time for learning, meeting with core constituents and on creative thinking (management excellence).

Notice how metrics fit into every one of the six core elements and even at the heart of how you manage the organization. Often, we think of numbers only when it comes to outcomes (programs) and finances (administration).

But metrics are applicable to all the core elements. By establishing measurable on-going evaluation and assessment strategies with embedded metrics across every aspect of the nonprofit, you will then have everything you need to develop strategic goals in the next important strategy in building sustainability: strategic planning.

Although the Total Quality Management (TQM) metric system for evaluation of for-profit business does not seem to be used as much now as it was several decades ago, it is a perfect example of a metric system of evaluation which cut across every aspect of a business. The TQM process required detailed measurements of the levels of quality in product development, administration, customer services, marketing, etc. The Core Elements Assessment is a simplified metric system that will compare board member and staff viewpoints on key aspects of the entire organization.

Two areas in administration are often big culprits when it comes to inadequate metrics: financial management and risk management. Four out of the five nonprofits where I served had serious financial management problems when I walked in the door as the new CEO. One of them had a $1.2 million deficit and the board did not know it. And now, as a consultant, I see it all the time in other nonprofits.

Nonprofits fail to allocate enough funding to hire good accounting staff and/or software and then wonder why they are unable to get good financial reports that meet the basic standards of accounting. How can you expect to build sustainability if you have no idea what is the financial health of your nonprofit?

Risk management issues can also trip up the administration of a nonprofit. By failing to adequately fund cybersecurity, for example, donor data and the private information of staff can get hacked, which can end up costing the organization more than just money to fix it. It will also cost time and the nonprofit's reputation. Not spending enough for adequate insurance coverage can also impact sustainability.

So, metrics is not just about statistical information, it is also about having in place the right policies and procedures in all the core elements to have the solid infrastructure to measure those numbers. Each of the books in *Nonprofit Management Simplified* series includes sample policies and procedures to help you build that solid infrastructure, an essential first step BEFORE metrics are useable. Addendum A is a checklist for policies and procedures development to help you decide what you might need to develop before establishing the needed metrics.

Strategy #4: Implement a Never-ending Strategic Planning Process

Mention the term "strategic planning" and you immediately think of a long, boring process resulting in a large binder of information that gets put on a shelf and never used. Never fear! I've simplified the process for you. It will not meet the rigors of a scientific, academically approved strategic planning process, but this award-winning, simplified process can jumpstart a never ending, gradually more sophisticated process that will engage both board and staff. The never-ending planning process will insure:

- There is a balance between all six of the core elements in your infrastructure,
- The nonprofit has established a clear and transformative vision and mission that drives everything you do,
- Metrics are embedded across all the six core elements to evaluate and assess the effectiveness of the established policies and procedures.

If your nonprofit is new to strategic planning, avoid hiring a consultant to do the planning for you, since then it becomes the consultant's plan, not yours. The process could be facilitated by an experienced consultant, but the plan must be developed by the board and senior staff.

A small nonprofit was told they needed a strategic plan to get a $100,000 grant. The ED had never done strategic planning. After talking to several colleagues, he recommended the board hire a local college professor who taught strategic planning. The price of $20,000 was steep, but the board agreed to take the money out of reserves to pay for it. When the consultant completed the plan, he walked into the ED's office, plopped a big notebook down on his desk and asked for his check. After the professor left, the ED started flipping through the notebook and discovered the plan was basically useless. There was nothing in the plan on volunteer development or fundraising. It turned out that the professor's classes were on strategic planning for for-profit businesses. The consultant knew nothing about nonprofits and the plan showed it.

The ED submitted the useless plan along with the grant request to the foundation, got the grant, and then put the plan on the shelf where it languished until the next ED threw it out.

An extreme example? Not really. Too many lengthy and sophisticated strategic planning processes are outdated by the time they are completed. But by using a simplified planning process that engages board and staff, and then updating it every year, strategic planning becomes a part of the culture of the organization and a key sustainability strategy. Why?

Because if staff, board members and everyone connected with the organization understands the direction and goals, they are more apt to give and be involved, thus increasing the possibility of long-term sustainability. Addendum B is an example of a simplified strategic plan.

In summary:

Building sustainability throughout the organization requires:

- A balanced approach in implementing all the core elements
- Establishing clear and transformative vision and mission statements
- Embedding metrics in all the core elements
- Implementing a never ending strategic planning process

Chapter Three

Establishing Sustainable Programs

Programs are the easiest core element of the nonprofit to illustrate how sustainability can be achieved. That's because programs are:
- The primary focus of most of the nonprofit's assets
- The basis for demonstrating results and outcomes measurements
- The focus of marketing and resource development campaigns
- How the mission of the nonprofit is implemented
- The most visible functions of the nonprofit.

For these reasons, and many more, program sustainability is an easy sell. Staff, volunteers, clients, the clients' families, donors and the community look at the results of your programs and become enthused about how they are changing lives and building a safe and healthy community.

Thus, they want what you are doing (programs) to continue and are willing to support it (resource development).

Many times, they don't know or don't care if the backroom operations are in shambles, if they see positive outcomes in the programs, at least not until it starts to impact the programs.

The reality is that unless those backroom operations (administration) as outlined in strategies #1-4 get their act together, it will eventually impact the ability of those programs to function effectively.

For now, let's assume the backroom operations are in fine shape. What are the specific sustainability strategies that programs need to implement to assure long-term sustainability? Let's look at two of the most critical strategies.

Strategy #5: Establish Outcomes Measurements

I'm always surprised when I find nonprofits still using statistics as their only measurement of success instead of outcomes. During one grant meeting, the funder asked a nonprofit ED why they should fund them. The ED said, "We provided food to 500 families last year." The funder then asked, "But what did you do to help those families becomes self-sufficient?"

A look of confusion appeared on the ED's face. Because she was unable to answer the question, the nonprofit did not receive funding. Why?

Because the funder wasn't interested in how many hungry people were fed, but rather how many people became self-sufficient.

Statistics indicate how many people were served by the programs (outputs), while outcomes indicate the results of being served. For example, a food bank might give food to 100 people each week (statistics), but outcomes would be 50 of those same people who received job training and are now employed and self-sufficient. And that's what the funder was looking for.

The development of an outcomes-based approach to programs is not something that happens overnight. There are several steps that are necessary before results can be measured. The *Nonprofit Management Simplified: Programs and Fundraising* book provides the details on how to develop this approach, so I will only cover the basics in this guide.

As you can see in Fig. 4, there are seven steps necessary for implementing an outcomes approach to measuring the effectiveness of your programs. DO NOT try to skip any of these steps. All of them are necessary. And, it will cost some money, so be sure to carefully consider the costs (staff, software, research, etc.) and allocate the funds before beginning the process.

It will be worth it in the long-run, since the return on investment will be great as your donors and potential donors understand the effectiveness of your programs.

Fig. 4: Steps for Implementing Outcomes Measurements

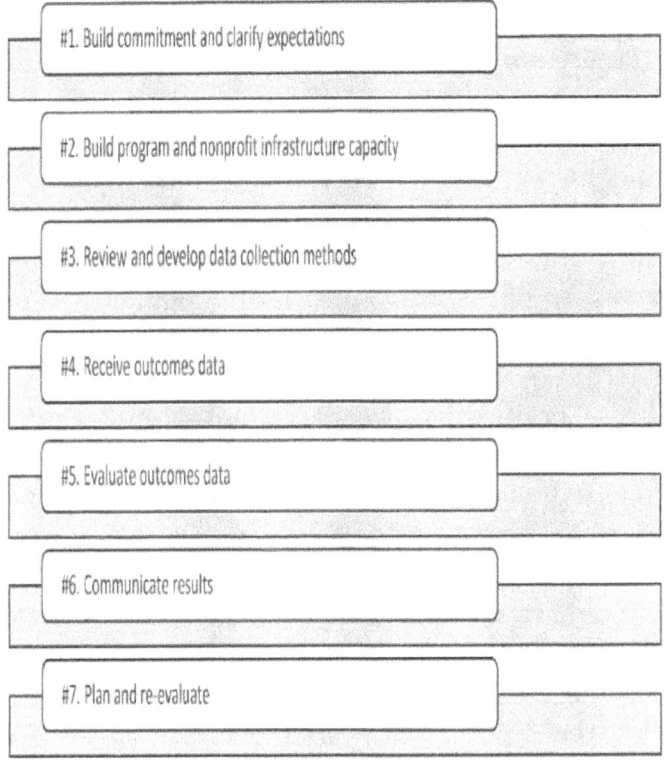

It might take at least a year before you will have accomplished steps #1-3, and then another couple of years before you have enough data from steps #4-5 before you can communicate results (step #6). But implementation of this outcomes measurements process greatly increases the possibilities for long-term sustainability of all your programs.

Strategy #6: Build Relevant Programs

It is only after you have established the outcomes measurements process that you will know whether the programs you are running are relevant (step #7). Only by carefully evaluating your programs and considering not only their effectiveness but their financial viability can you determine if they are worth continuing. Too often nonprofits keep running the same programs, simply because clients continue to be involved, not because they are necessarily effective.

The easiest example of this is a typical after-school activities program. Let's assume that the program provides after-school recreational activities, such as different types of sports. Children and youth have been involved for years, primarily because of the social activity and it is something to do after school.

But let's compare the differences between this type of after-school recreational activity, with no outcomes measurements, and a more relevant approach.

An after-school program established an outcomes measurements strategy and discovered during the research phase that more than half of the children involved in their recreational program were reading at below grade level. So, the nonprofit implemented a one-hour tutoring program that children were required to attend before they could participate in the recreation. Within two years, the reading level of 80% of the children who had been reading below their grade level was at or above grade level. Now they had a relevant program that was more than just about keeping the children occupied. This is a relevant, positive, program outcomes measurement.

Do you see the difference between a program and a relevant program? The relevant program is based on evaluation and outcomes measurements. And relevant programs will be able to change to meet the needs of the clients and the community.

Being able to clearly identify measurable, positive outcomes for programs and then adapt and change programs to make them relevant to the needs of the clients and to the community, means it is more likely the nonprofit and the programs will be sustainable.

<u>In summary:</u>

Increasing the possibility that a nonprofit's programs will be sustainable will require:
   a. The establishment of an outcomes measurements process,
   b. The ability to change and adapt with relevant programs.

Chapter Four

Implementing a Sustainable Resource Development Program

Resource development is the life blood of any nonprofit. Without adequate funding, regardless of how relevant or viable the programs, no matter how positive the outcomes, the nonprofit will not be sustainable. We all know this, but we constantly struggle to procure adequate funding. Resource development is broadly defined as all the resources needed to support and fund the nonprofit, including staff, volunteers, equipment, facilities, reserves, programs, insurance, cyber security, supplies, etc.

In chapter three I discussed the importance of metrics in resource development. For example, knowing how many repeat donors you have and whether they are increasing their contributions. There are other excellent resources available on every aspect of fundraising. Even a quick search on the Internet or Amazon will produce hundreds of books on the subject by field-tested professionals.

In this chapter I will focus on two specific strategies for building a sustainable resource development program, not just building your donor base. I have not only experienced the struggles associated with fundraising, but I have observed two broad resource development strategies that if implemented will determine if a nonprofit will be sustainable over a long period:
1. Diversification of funding sources
2. Constant evaluation of fundraising costs compared to fundraising income.

Strategy #7: Diversify Funding Sources

Before we get into the meat of this strategy, I recommend you pull some resource development records from your accounting records. Put them together in charts like figures #5 and #6.

The first chart, Fig. 5, shows what your fundraising might look like as a percentage of your total income over a four-year period. In this chart for a hypothetical nonprofit, government grants for 2015 were 30% of the total income, while on-line donations decreased to less than 3%.

By looking at these numbers for the past four to five years you can get an idea of what is working and what is not working, where the declines in resource development are occurring, and where the nonprofit is seeing increases.

Where are the areas where you might be able to focus attention, and increase resources? Too often we keep using the same strategies and wonder why we keep getting the same results.

But there is another advantage of a chart like this: being able to see at a glance if more than 20% of your funding is coming from any single source. That is a critical issue if you are trying to build sustainability. The greater your dependency on a single source of income, the less sustainable your nonprofit will be. In the example, too much funding is coming from government grants. And government grants are notorious for suddenly drying up, depending on how the political winds are blowing. If 30% of your funding was suddenly cut off what would you do? How could you keep the programs going? Do you have adequate reserves to cover such a drastic reduction in funding?

Do you see how an annual analysis of your resource development sources is so critical? This exercise might also jumpstart a discussion with your board on the need to develop a planned giving program, either through a local community foundation or by starting your own foundation. By the way, I always recommend working with the local community foundation rather than starting your own foundation.

That's because starting a foundation requires a high level of expertise in planned-giving and investments, plus it takes several years to establish a viable foundation. It requires less of a drain on a nonprofit's resources to work with a community foundation than to start your own.

Fig. 5: Fundraising as Percentage of Total Income

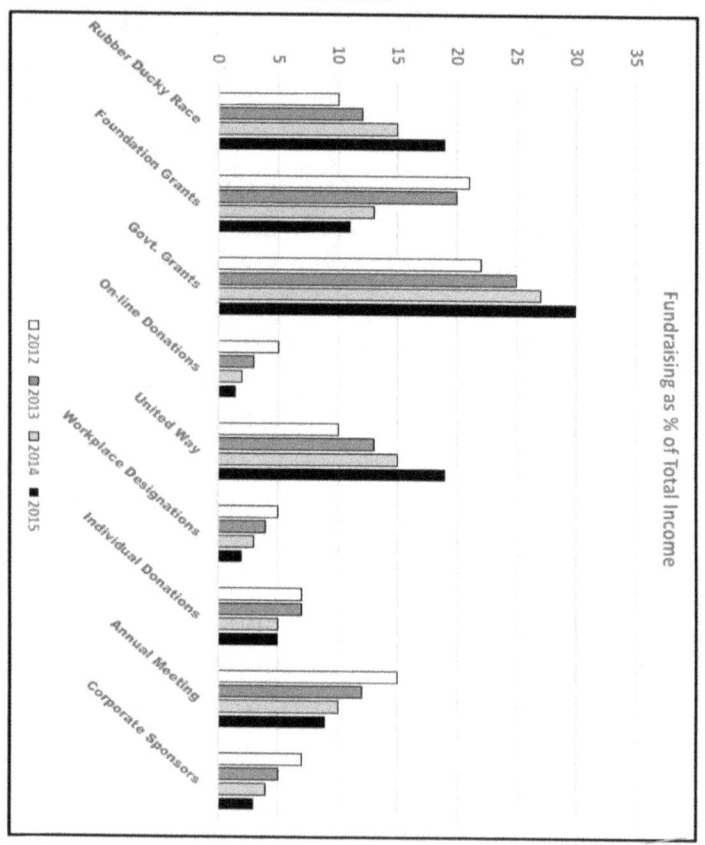

Or maybe there is a need to focus on developing high-end donors to build up a reserve fund. Regardless of how you address the issue, sustainability in resource development requires a hard look at how you are diversifying your funding sources. The goal should always be to never have more than 20% of your funding coming from any single source.

Strategy #8: Evaluate Fundraising Costs vs. Fundraising Income

One of the nonprofits where I worked had an annual Rubber Ducky race. Every year for ten years, people in the community would excitedly buy a small rubber duck that had a number printed on the bottom. Then the thousands of ducks purchased were dumped into the local river where they were eventually herded into a channel while the crowds on the riverbank cheered on their duck. The first duck through the channel won a car for their owner.

Sounds like fun and a great fundraiser, right? But there were some problems. Over the years, the name of the nonprofit had become so subsumed by the title "Rubber Ducky Race" that a market survey showed most people had no idea where the money was going from the proceeds.

The second big problem was that the cost of staff time (which was not added to the actual expenses) and the expenses of the race had become so great that we were lucky if we ended up with $1,000 when it was all done.

Unfortunately, the board of directors so loved the idea of the race they were unwilling to either turn it over to another organization or end the money-draining, staff-consuming event.

So, another issue to consider when looking at your resource development program is the costs associated with all your fundraising events and strategies compared to the income you are generating. And do not forget to include in those costs staff time. Failure to include staff time in those costs means you do not have an accurate picture of what it is costing the organization to run the event or collect the funds. Keeping accurate records for staff time is not only a fundraising issue, but also impacts overhead costs. If, for example, the ED is not separating out the time he/she spends on fundraising or programs, all the ED's salary and benefits will be allocated to administration, wrongly inflating the overall administrative costs. This illustrates another reason why the backroom operations must be done correctly, otherwise it can have a negative impact on the overall organization and, in the long run, on sustainability issues.

Fig. 6 is an example of a comparison of fundraising costs to income. Notice that while the costs of the rubber ducky race went down in 2015, look at how high they were in the previous year; and the chart does not show actual staff costs. Why did the costs go down and are they apt to be up or down in the future? Grant costs for 2015 are also high. The goal is to keep fundraising costs below 15%. Many nonprofits unrealistically try to keep fundraising costs below 8%, but is that possible? It takes money to raise money so don't avoid resource development strategies that could help build sustainability (such as planned giving), just because they might have some up-front costs. Planned giving programs can take several years to implement and usually require the hiring of at least one full-time staff person, but it can take several years before the nonprofit sees a return on their investment.

These issues of fundraising and administrative costs should generate some discussions about the common myths associated with them. I frequently hear board members and staff talk about how critical it is that fundraising costs be kept to 7.5% and overhead also at 7.5%, for a total of 15%. But is that realistic? Who decided those percentages were adequate to raise the necessary funds to keep the nonprofit solvent and sustainable?

Obviously, there is a need to avoid overinflated percentages for fundraising and administration, but too often we shoot ourselves in the foot by unrealistic demands for these percentages. What should those percentages be for the nonprofit to be sustainable in the long-term? Can you justify higher percentages to your donors? If you can, then don't back down but rather speak forcefully for your organization to the board and donors about the outcomes, not the overhead.

Fig. 6: Fundraising Costs vs. Fundraising Income

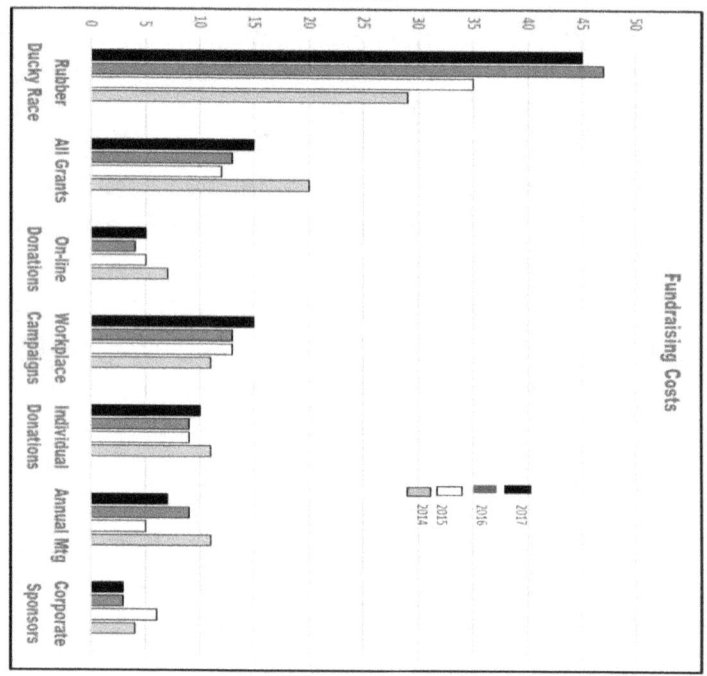

In summary:
Sustainability strategies in resource development include:
1. Diversification of funding sources,
2. Frequent evaluation of fundraising costs vs. income.

Chapter 5

Developing Administration Strategies to Support Sustainability

There are four key strategies within the administration core element which are essential for building sustainability within the nonprofit:
1. Implement a senior staff succession plan and policies
2. Establish institutional memory procedures
3. Implement accelerating technologies
4. Outsource when it is feasible.

While many of the basic infrastructure sustainability strategies dealt with in chapter one are the responsibility of the administration department or division, these four additional strategies must also be implemented within the department to assure sustainability.

Strategy #9: Implement a Senior Staff Succession Plan and Policies

Because the turnover rate among nonprofit staff is often high because of low salaries and stress, with staff only staying two to three years, the development of succession plans for senior staff is critical. Otherwise, you may just get a staff person trained – which usually takes a year – when they receive a better offer and are gone. Then you must start all over.

So why not have in place the policies and procedures to quickly bring new staff up to date on their responsibilities, or have someone already on staff prepared to step into the position?

Long-term sustainability increases as such policies are implemented, since the transition to new staff leadership is much smoother.

Let's begin with the process of developing an ED succession plan. Before developing a succession plan or strategy, the ED needs to answer the following questions:

- How long do you intend to stay in the position?
- How well would the nonprofit function if something were to happen to you that made it impossible for you to be the ED (e.g. death or serious illness or injury)?
- Which employee would be able to step into your place as an interim ED?
- Has the board considered a succession plan?
- Will an interim ED be needed?

Once the ED has answered these questions, write a one or two paragraph statement that best expresses your views on a succession plan (Fig.7), and then take it to the board for their review. It should be noted that many ED's are hesitant to take this step because they are afraid that if the board looks at this issue they will decide it is time for a new ED. However, if the ED handles this issue correctly, it will not only provide guidance to the board, but it might trigger valid reasons why it is time for the ED to move to another nonprofit, or why the ED needs an increase in salary.

Look at each of the senior staff positions and ask similar questions and then develop a similar succession policy for the other senior staff.

Fig. 7: ED Succession Policy

To diminish the potential negative impact on the nonprofit in the event of the sudden departure of the executive director (ED), the board has adopted the following succession plan policy:

The ED will provide training to the associate director on the management responsibilities of the ED, based on the job description. In the event the ED is no longer able to fulfill their duties or resigns, the associate director will serve as the interim director until the board completes the board-approved search process and a new ED is hired.

Strategy #10: Establish Institutional Memory Procedures

When there is a mass exodus of staff, especially in smaller organizations, institutional memory often departs with them. Institutional memory means not only the "how" or the way things are done within the organization, but can also apply to critical contacts within the community. When these contacts are lost, especially the names of important donors, it can take a long time to recover the data and to renew the contacts. This is especially true if the nonprofit lacks a good donor database which is regularly updated. In some cases, when an ED has served in their position for several decades and suddenly dies, even the details related to the history of the organization can be lost if they were never written down.

So how do you guarantee instituional memory is not lost and continues? One of the best ways is for the staff to annually develop or review a policies and procedures manual. Preferably the manual would be on a computer, with off-site or Cloud backups, categorized by the various departments of the nonprofit, or by the core elements as in Fig. 2.

If the nonprofit does not yet have such a manual, it will take some time to put it together. I know because this is one of the first things I did at every organization where I served. I did this for two reasons:

1. To learn how things were done within the organization,
2. To put in writing the institution's memory and history.

I did not do all the work myself, but asked each staff person to take time each day, usually an hour, to methodically write down exactly what they did and how they did it. They tied this in with their job description, too. Interestingly enough, this exercise not only helped them crystalize their job duties and helped me to better understand everyone's jobs, but it sometimes identified where there were needs for more staff or overlapping duties. The policies and procedures manual checklist in Addendum A can provide a starting point for the types of things that need to be included.

In some cases, when a long serving ED left, I had to sit down with the ED or long-term volunteers and actually write a history of the nonprofit. This became a valuable marketing tool, especially if there was a critical milestone in the nonprofit's history coming up, like a 25th or 50th anniversary of its founding.

Strategy #11: Implement Acelerating Technologies

Unfortunately, too many nonprofits are stuck using someone elses hand-me-downs, or outdated technology, unwilling or unable to spend the needed funds to upgrade. But I've seen what can happen to nonprofits who keep up with the accelerated rates of improving technologies and to those who do not. And that includes making sure there are people on staff or contracted to keep all of the software and technology working and constantly updated.

CAUTION: Do not use a volunteer as your technology person, just because it is less expensive. That's because you often have no idea what are the qualifications of the person and also because they may not be up to date on the latest software and cyber security issues.

A food bank in Orlando, Florida, set up up a phenominal assembly line warehouse for the receipt and disbursement of donations of food. It is so efficient that it now supplies food to dozens of other food banks in central Florida. Using technology, the nonprofit is able to process even perishable donations quickly and efficiently. Through their database they know which food banks need which types of donations and their fleet of trucks move the inventory quickly so it gets to them before it can spoil.

Did it cost money to set it up? Sure. But both the board and senior staff had the foresight to recognize the value of spending the money up front on the technology in order to not only serve more food banks, and ultimately more hungry families, but at the same time increase their sustainability.

One of the ways this improved technology increased their sustainability was that corporate donors like major grocery stores saw the long-term value of the accelerated technology and helped to fund it. And they continued to fund needed upgrades, indicating their commitment to sustaining the food bank.

In contrast, another nonprofit is struggling to exist because the board is unwilling to spend the money on a desperately needed donor database software that will interface with the accounting software. Instead, they will have to pay for an extra staff person to enter donor data into the donor database and then enter information by hand into the accounting software, which by the way is only using a small business accounting package instead of a more sophisticated software package. The result is that the nonprofit will actually end up spending more time and money on staff. And, even then, there is no guarantee the donor data entered into the accounting software will be correct because the only way to verify the information entered is to check it by hand.

Another area of missed opportunity in technology for many nonprofits is in facilities management.

Many nonprofits own their own facilties. Tony Keane, president and CEO of the International Facility Management Association said, "Studies show that the initial cost of (facilities) development accounts for only 15% to 20% of the life-cycle cost of a facility. The biggest chunk comes from continuing asset management."

Building automation systems can greatly reduce the costs and make for more enviornmentally friendly buildings, besides promoting community good will. This includes everything from security systems, window treatments, and low-flush toilets to solar systems and how they might impact the bottom line and economic sustainability. And don't forget the issue of meeting disability requirements.

Finally, nonprofits MUST build secure data systems to protect donor, client, staff and volunteer data. The question is not "if" you will be hacked, but "when." Unless a nonprofit has a plan in place accelerating their database security systems to protect themselves one instance of hacking could have a devestating impact on the organization, making sustainability impossible because of lawsuits. Developing your risk management plan and keeping it updated, especially as it relates to technology, is essential.

The nonprofit who sees implementing constantly accelerating technologies throughout every facet of the organization as absolutely essential – and is willing to budget for it – is more apt to be sustainable in the long-run.

Strategy #12: Outsource What you Can

When the board of directors of my fourth non-profit suggested we outsource our payroll functions, I was skeptical at first. I was used to handling all of the human resources (HR) functions in house and I wasn't sure how it would work. But, after studying it carefully with a cost benefit analysis, I was surprised at how much it could save us.

We were getting ready to hire someone to handle all of the HR functions, but by outsourcing everything it ended up costing us less money than it would have to hire a full-time staff person. Not only that, but due to all of the constantly changing legal issues associated with HR, it greatly reduced the need for me as the CEO to keep up with labor laws since the HR company would handle everything.

It also meant that regardless of what happened with our staff, there would be a company outside of ours with the institutional memory on all things related to HR.

And, remember, any time you implement a strategy that enhances institutional memory it can increase sustainability.

Besides HR functions, there are other administrative functions that can be outsourced, depending on the needs of the nonprofit. Such as:

- Research for outcomes measurements through a local college
- Planned giving through a local community foundation
- Volunteer recruitment through a local nonprofit resource center
- Marketing through a local public relations firm
- Facilities management through a property management company
- Accounting functions by a Certified Public Accountant
- Cyber security by an expert in the field (not a local volunteer)
- Grant writing (by an experienced consultant)
- Facilitation of strategic planning, board training, etc. (by an experienced consultant).

These are just a few ideas of ways you can increase sustainability by outsourcing. When you hire experts outside your nonprofit to handle these functions you often get highly qualified services for less than what it would cost if you tried to fill the position in-house.

Not only that, by hiring experts in their fields, you often gain new and objective perspectives that increase sustainability possibilities. When you have these services provided on a contract basis always be sure there are specific parameters within the contract as to who does what and when. Always get references before signing any contract and do your homework to make sure they will do what they say they will do. Compare the cost of outsourcing to doing it in-house. Include penalties for failure to accomplish tasks within designated timeframes. Remember, just because you are contracting for a service doesn't mean you don't have to monitor them!

<u>In summary</u>:

Increasing sustainability in your administrative functions will be achieved through:

    1. Implementation of senior staff succession plans and proceedures,
    2. The establishment of institutional memory procedures,
    3. Implementation of accelerating technologies,
    4. Outsourcing certain administrative functions.

Chapter Six

Developing Sustainablity Strategies in the Board and Volunteer Development Program

It constantly amazes me how few nonprofits have volunteer development coordinators, yet may have hundreds or thousands of volunteers. Instead they regard volunteers as an irritating necessity rather than as a positive resource, failing to understand all the positives volunteers can bring to their organization, especially when it comes to building sustainability.

A quick history lesson. Volunteers have always been the life's blood of the United States of America. The Frenchman, Alexis deTouquville, traveled the USA in the early 1800s, observing and writing about the incredible volunteer spirit that was building the new country.

Even today, no other country in the world has volunteerism so deeply embedded within its culture.

Millions of our citizens volunteer regularly to build homes for the homeless, care for the sick, feed the hungry, support youth programs, strive to save the enviornment, and so much more.

Yet, even with willing volunteers, too often the nonprofits where they serve fail to build solid policies and procedures related to recruitment, training, recogntion and dismissal of the three types of volunteers: board members, committee members and program volunteers. You can find sample policies and procedures in the *Nonprofit Management Simplified* books.

In this guide, I will instead focus on three distinct sustainability strategies within the board and volunteer development program, based on the assumption you already have a formal program. If you don't have one, go to the book, implement the program, and then come back and take a look at these three strategies:

 1. Implement a volunteer succession plan,
 2. Establish regular board training,
 3. Recruit high capacity volunteers.

Strategy #13: Implement a Volunteer Succession Plan

Remember in the last chapter the discussion about building institutional memory? The same rational is behind the need for implementing a volunteer succession plan.

This is particularly important within small to mid-sized nonprofits. Larger organizations generally do not rely as heavily on volunteers so volunteer succession planning may not be as important. However, even in very large nonprofits, the development of successions plans for the top leadership of the board of directors is important.

So how do you develop a volunteer succession plan? Basically it involves a three-step process.

Step #1: Identify the volunteer positions where a succession plan is necessary

In order to do this, first identify the types of volunteers who are involved within your organization. Generally, there are five types of volunteers:

- Board members – Depending on the governance structure, these are unpaid volunteers who are recruited to serve for a specific term of office. They are usually selected for their expertise in a particular field, for their knowledge of the community, or because they have contributed a significant amount of money to the nonprofit. Board members meet monthly or quarterly and are legally liable for the decisions they make or do not make. Their duties are outlined in the bylaws of the nonprofit.

- <u>Committee members</u> – Boards will often have standing committees for each of the core elements (Fig. 2). Usually the chair and vice-chair are board members but other committee members can include residents from within the community with a high level of expertise in the focus area of the committee. For example, the marketing committee might include representatives from public relations or marketing firms. Because the purpose of the committees is to draft policies to take to the board for approval and to advise the staff in a particular area, they have no legal standing. Some boards require that every board member serve on a committee.
- <u>Program volunteers</u> – Some board members may choose to also be program volunteers, under the direction of staff running specific programs. For example, the staff in charge of resource development might recruit board members to help with a golf tournament. As program volunteers the board members serve as unpaid staff. Program volunteers do a myriad of tasks and do not have to be board members. They can stuff envelopes, help at a daycare, serve food at a soup kitchen, help build a house, or speak with legislators about upcoming legislation.

- <u>Virtual volunteers</u> – More and more nonprofits are realizing the value of incorporating into their volunteer programs off-site volunteers. These types of volunteers can often do data entry and other administrative tasks from their home. Sometimes they have a disability, but other times the nonprofit doesn't have office space so it is more economical for the volunteer to work from home. Some types of virtual volunteer duties are included in Fig.8.
- <u>Volunteers with disabilities</u> – It is estimated 20% of the residents in any community have some type of disability, making them a huge, often untapped volunteer resource. Because these individuals deal with daily struggles just to survive, they are usually extremely resilient and make great volunteers.

Regardless of the types of volunteers involved with your nonprofit, there will be challenges like communication, attitudes of staff, performance reviews and the need for specific policies and procedures to protect everyone.

Rarely would there be a need for a succession plan for program volunteers. That is because they serve under staff direction.

Fig. 8– Examples of Virtual Volunteer Duties

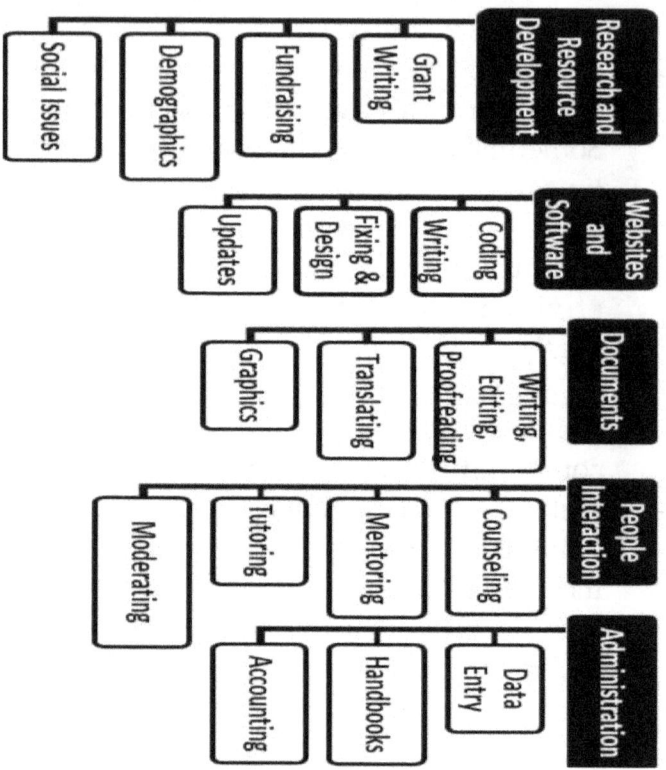

However, in smaller nonprofits with no staff, or few staff, if a program volunteer is in charge of a golf tournament, for example, it might make sense for the event committee to appoint a successor to plan for the next year's tournament.

However, the leadership of committees could benefit from a succession plan since their work will continue from year to year and institutional memory is important to keep them on track.

In the same way, board members and officers of the board need to have succession plans. Too often nominating committees wait until a month before the annual election, meet, struggle to find someone to fill the positions and then hope to have a slate to present to the board for the election. How much easier it would be if they had succession plans in place to provide continuity in the volunteer leadership of the organization.

Step #2: Develop the Plan

For purposes of this guide, I will focus on succession plans for board-level committees and the board, not program volunteers.

The easiest succession plan for committees is to simply make sure at the beginning of each fiscal year that a vice-chair for the committee is appointed, with the understanding that not only will the vice-chair fill in for the chair when he/she is absent, but they will be willing to step into the chair's position the next year.

If the job descriptions for both positions are written in this way, then everyone knows the succession plan when they accept the position.

Sample job descriptions for the chair and vice chair of a committee are included as Addendum C.

Board members generally serve for set terms: three two-year terms or two three-year terms. The bylaws of the nonprofit will specify those terms. Succession for the board terms is generally decided by a nominating committee or volunteer development committee, either when the board member's term is up, or if they resign.

Officers of the board of directors are recommended by the nominating committee or volunteer development committee as well. Again, the bylaws of the nonprofit will specify the method of election and their terms of office. Terms of office are best for no more than two years. The rationale for this is to avoid power struggles and encourage new ideas by rotating officers every year or every two years. Potential succession plans for officers might be:

- Past chair, succeeded by the previous year's board chair
- Board chair, succeeded by the vice chair
- Vice chair, succeeded by one of the committee chairs
- Treasurer, succeeded by the chair of the Finance or Administration Committee
- Secretary, succeeded by the chair of the Administration Committee

There is a big advantage to having the officers selected from the chairs of the committees, since they will have served at least one year in a position that gives them opportunities to get to know the staff, board members and the organization before moving into an officer position.

Some nonprofits try to develop board chair succession plans that go up to five years out. Such a succession plan for a board chair might look like this:

- 2016 Chair of the Finance Committee (or one of the other committees)
- 2017 Treasurer (or Secretary)
- 2018 Vice Chair of the Board
- 2019 Chair of the Board
- 2020 Past Chair of the Board

This type of succession planning insures high levels of knowledge and commitment on the part of the most important volunteer leadership position within the organization: the chair of the board. However, it is very important that any succession plan be subject to annual review by the nominating committee or volunteer development committee.

This is because sometimes a behavioral issue may show up in someone when they are serving at the committee level that would cause the nominating committee to question whether or not they are fit to serve as the board chair.

Or, illness or job transfers might interfere with the five-year plan. Everyone at every level (volunteers and staff) must understand that any succession plan is subject to change. This should be specified in all the officer job descriptions, as shown in Addendum D.

Avoid the trap of trying to recuit board chairs solely based on their importance within the community. This is because these are often very busy people and cannot commit the three to five years necessary for a good succession plan. And the advantages of having a high-profile individual as the board chair are a lot less than the advantages of a good succession plan.

Step #3: Implement the Plan

Implementation of any succession plan is pretty straight forward. However, be sure you have in place a dismissal policy in the event a volunteer either fails to fulfill the duties specified in their job description, is disruptive or the nominating committee determines they are unfit to serve. Sample dismissal policies are included in *Nonprofit Management Simplified: Board and Volunteeer Development*.

Developing this type of volunteer succession plan greatly improves sustainability of the nonprofit by increasing the institutional memory and providing continuity within the leadership.

Strategy #14: Establish Regular Board Training

Have your board members said to you, "I don't need board training?" Chances are those board members are the ones who DO need training. Here's why. Most board members have no idea what they don't know. They have sat on boards for years and yet have no clue what their legal governance responsibilities are. And, too often the ED doesn't understand their roles either. So, board meetings can become either a waste of time or opportunities for board members to control or micromanage the ED, not to mention how few board members know how to run effective meetings.

Building a culture of regular board training can be difficult. However, it is one of the most important strategies for building sustainability. It is only when the board members understand their roles, responsibilities and lines of authority in relationship to staff that they can govern as they are supposed to.

The chart in Fig. 9 illustrates the correct relationships between board and staff, regardless of which "hat" a board member is wearing. When a board member is serving in their governance role as a board member, wearing their legal hat, the only staff responsible to them is the ED.

But when that same board member is serving on a committee, there are no lines of authority. The staff advises the committee and the committee advises the staff. When the board member is serving food at the soup kitchen, working at a fundraiser, or stuffing envelopes as a program volunteer, the designated staff person is the supervisor of the board member. So many communication difficulties between board members and staff could be avoided if this chart were included in every new board member orientation and then referred to when there are problems.

But board training is not just about orientation when a new board member is selected, sustainable organizations include regular training at board meetings and at annual board retreats. For example, each board meeting could include five to ten minutes of education on a topic, such as the simplified parliamentary procedure (Addendum E), how to conduct an effective meeting, or a myriad of other topics related to their role as a board member.

Another interesting topic for a mini-training for board members are the various nonprofit board governance models.

Too often nonprofits fail to understand that as the nonprofit grows the board may need to move away from a more administrative style of governance to a more hands-off style of governance, as discussed in *Nonprofit Management Simplified: Board and Volunteer Development.*

Fig. 9: Board & Staff Roles, Responsibilities & Lines of Authority

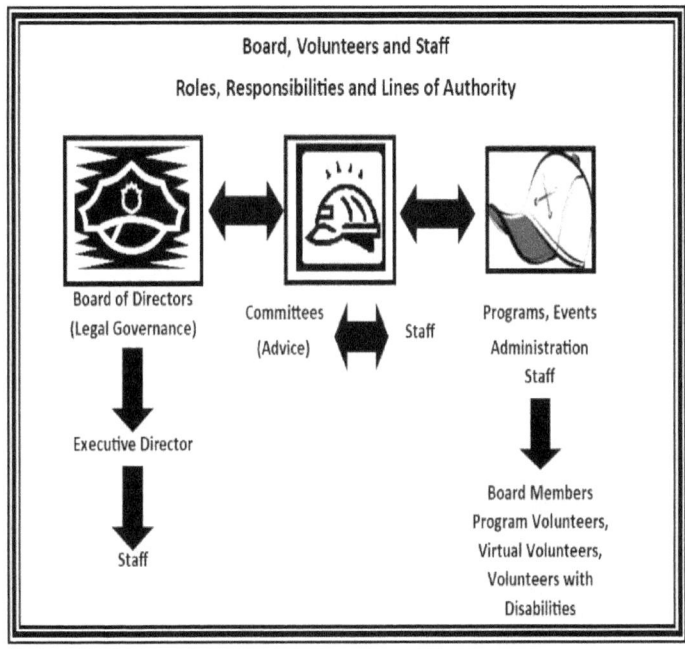

Building a culture of on-going board training is critical for building a sustainable nonprofit. It is only when board members are up-to-date on their governance roles will they be able to grow with the organization. There are a wide range of types of trainings:
- Mini-trainings at board meetings
- Two-hour facilitated trainings with an outside consultant
- Board retreats, with a focus on a specific area of governance or a risk management issue
- Board training coupled with the simplified strategic planning process outlined in chapter one
- One-on-one trainings/orientations for new board members
- A buddy system whereby a new board member is mentored by a veteran board member
- An on-line webinar style of training (available on my website).

Strategy #15: Recruit High-Capacity Volunteers

Whether it is for the board of directors, committees or as program volunteers, high-capacity volunteers bring an added level of expertise and knowledge to any non-profit and can increase sustainability. What do I mean by "high-capacity?"

The term has been coined to refer to a highly-educated and experienced volunteer who maybe has just retired and is looking for community service opportunities. These types of volunteers truly are looking for challenging work within your nonprofit, not just stuffing envelopes. High-capacity means the volunteer has a high level of knowledge or expertise they want to use for the benefit of your nonprofit and the community.

Unless you are prepared to work with them, you will lose them. Let me illustrate. A former nonprofit executive retired and decided she wanted to volunteer in the new community she and her husband had moved to. Over a period of three years she applied to several nonprofits, offering to serve. Not one of them ever called her back after she completed all the applications, including criminal background checks. Puzzled, she tried to follow-up and here is what she found out, second-hand, from one of them: "Oh, our ED doesn't want you volunteering with us because with all your experience you intimidate him." Undoubtedly the other nonprofit ED's felt the same way.

Those nonprofits lost what could have been an extremely valuable, high-capacity volunteer because they had no idea how to incorporate her experience and talents into the organization. How sad.

And this is where we get back to the whole concept of a volunteer development program as we discussed in strategy #13. To recruit and retain high-capacity volunteers be sure you already have in place the policies and procedures for recruitment, training, recognition and dismissal.

Because high capacity volunteers are so knowledgeable they will recognize a half-hearted, shoddy volunteer development program in a flash and will not want to be associated with it. On the other hand, a high-capacity volunteer might be just the right person to organize your volunteer development program.

Don't forget that volunteers are often the best donors. So, when you engage a high-capacity volunteer fully, they will be more apt to give. And, because they will often have a higher level of wealth, they have the potential to participate in planned giving programs, too.

Suffice it to say, by developing your volunteer program so you consciously recruit high-capacity volunteers you will build sustainability by increasing the level of expertise in your volunteer program while at the same time adding funds to your resource development coffers.

Just be sure that you do not fall into the trap of trying to replace staff with high-capacity volunteers.

Not only will the other staff resent it, but you could run into legal trouble if the staff person they replaced decides to file a lawsuit for unfair labor practices.

In summary:

Build sustainability in your board and volunteer development program by:
1. Implementing a volunteer succession plan,
2. Establishing regular board training,
3. Recruiting high-capacity volunteers.

Chapter 7

Implementing Sustainability in the Marketing Program

Marketing within many nonprofits is viewed as publicity for events, or something tagged on "if we have money for it." However, a solid marketing program can have a profound, positive impact on the entire organization when it is done right, building a more sustainable nonprofit.

Two marketing strategies will help build sustainability within your organization:
1. Integrate marketing throughout the entire organization,
2. Demonstrate value to the community through building brand identity.

Strategy 16: Integrate Marketing throughout the Organization

If your nonprofit is like most, marketing is reserved for publication of fundraising events. Let's see if I can change your thinking about marketing by looking at it as a tool for building sustainability. Let me illustrate.

Suppose you had discovered the cure for cancer through a vaccine. Would you only celebrate that knowledge with the patients and families of those who benefited from your cure? Of course, not. You would want everyone to know so that everyone could benefit. Not only might future patients need to know about the cure, but you would need additional funding to support disbursement of this miracle vaccine. And that's where marketing would be essential.

In the same way, your nonprofit has a vision and a mission. Hopefully you have proven outcomes measurements that clearly demonstrate the successes of your programs. You want other potential clients to benefit and you need additional funding to support expansion of the program for those potential clients. You have embedded metrics throughout the organization (strategy #3). You need a marketing program.

But marketing is not just about the exciting programs you run. Marketing is a strategy that, when used properly, highlights all the other five core elements of your nonprofit:

1. <u>Administration</u>
- Your solid financial position,
- Your protection of donor, staff and client information (risk management),
- The well-run facility,

- The human resources department that meets all legal requirements and attracts only the best staff,
- The latest accelerating technologies to help meet the demands of the nonprofit.

2. <u>Board and volunteer development</u>
- The exciting volunteer development program you have,
- The high-capacity volunteers donating time and money,
- The awards your volunteers have won.

3. <u>Resource development</u>
- The wonderful events you sponsor that raise money for the nonprofit,
- The leadership giving program,
- The gifts-in-kind program,
- The planned-giving program.

4. <u>Programs</u>
- The proven, outcomes-based programs with measurements showing their success in clients' lives,
- The creative, ever-changing programs adapting to the needs of the clients.

5. <u>Community Involvement</u>
- The leadership role the organization plays within the community around the issue that drives your mission and demonstrates value,
- The collaborative efforts to solve community problems and leverage assets.

When you look at marketing as a strategy to develop ways to highlight everything the nonprofit is doing right, not just programs and fundraising, it suddenly becomes a totally integrated strategy to build long-term sustainability.

Strategy #17: Demonstrate Value to the Community

When marketing is integrated across every facet of the nonprofit, it becomes easy to demonstrate value to the community and build brand identity. Brand identity is loosely defined as what sets your nonprofit apart from other nonprofits in the community. The book, *Nonprofit Management Simplified: Programs and Fundraising,* includes a chapter on marketing and building brand identity by showing you how to determine which brand fits your organization.

But it isn't just about determining brand identity to build sustainability, you must be able to show the community that what you are doing is valuable. Sure, outcomes measurements can demonstrate value to your clients, but how to do you demonstrate value to the wider community?

Let's go back to the difference between outputs (statistics) and outcomes (measurements), as discussed in strategy #5. One of the best marketing examples of outcomes is Heifer International, a nonprofit providing animals to citizens in third world countries.

Their basic values statement is:

Giving an animal is like giving someone a small business, providing wool, milk, eggs and more. Animal donations can provide families a hand up, increasing access to medicine, school, food and a sustainable livelihood.

Their website then shows pictures of individuals with various animals, indicating what it costs to buy an animal or contribute a share of an animal. For example, a goat costs $120, while a goat "share" is $10.

The entire marketing campaign of Heifer International demonstrates tangible value to the communities where their clients live. When their clients build self-sufficiency with their animals and then can sell the produce from the animals, they can put money back into their community, supporting other businesses. This cycle of value to the community starts, in this case, with just one goat.

Building sustainability within your nonprofit requires some careful thought about the value-add to your community. What is that you are doing that adds value to the community? Are you making the community safer or healthier? How do you convey that value to the community? If you cannot demonstrate value with your marketing, then sustainability will eventually become an issue.

<u>In summary</u>:

Marketing strategies are critical to building a sustainable nonprofit. Two important marketing strategies for building sustainability are:
1. Integration of marketing throughout the entire organization,
2. Demonstrating value to the community.

Chapter Eight

Expanding Community Involvement

It is easy to become so focused on what we are doing within our organization that we forget about the world outside our doors. To ignore the community around us is a recipe for eventual disaster. Building sustainability requires expanding your involvement within the community. Sometimes "community" will simply be your neighborhood, but usually it means the wider sphere which your nonprofit impacts and which impacts you.

For example, every nonprofit is affected by what happens in local, state and national governments, but too often we ignore what they are doing because we do not want to jeopardize our nonprofit status for fear of being accused of lobbying. The language used about nonprofit lobbying is very vague, with terms like "no substantial portion" of the assets being used for lobbying.

Many nonprofits will, therefore, set aside no more than 20% of their ED's time to lobby government officials on statutes or bills which may impact their ability to serve their clients. Another way to increase lobbying impact is to have board members contact government officials to let them know your organization's position on issues. Since they are volunteers they can do so without impacting the lobbying limitations on the organization.

When I was serving at a nonprofit in Texas, one of the state legislators proposed a bill that would have required all the board members of every nonprofit in the state be selected by public election.

If the nonprofits had not been paying attention to what was going on and the bill had passed, it could have had incredibly far-reaching impact on the sector. The bill never made it to committee, once the nonprofit sector marshalled their incredible resources and let the other legislators know how ridiculous and expensive the proposal was.

This is just one example of how important community involvement can be. There are three strategies related to this area that can help you build sustainability:

1. Build competitive advantage
2. Leverage assets through collaboration
3. Establish your leadership role in your primary mission.

Strategy #18: Build Competitive Advantage

I am amazed how many times someone approaches me about starting a nonprofit without first checking to see if there is anyone else in the community already doing what they propose. One of the most common start-ups in a community is a food bank. But in most communities, they are often dozens of food banks. Does the area need another one?

Without a doubt, most individuals who want to start a nonprofit have the passion to serve and want to make a difference in their community. But it is also true that very few of them do their homework before they file for their 501(c)3 nonprofit status with the Internal Revenue Service (IRS). And that is precisely why there is often duplication of services in most communities. I always advise these start-ups to go through a set of questions BEFORE they file to become a nonprofit to make sure there is a need for the services they are proposing.

I have been involved in needs and resource assessments in every community where I have served. The number one problem in every community was not "lack of resources" but rather, "don't know where the resources are." T

This is precisely why local United Ways have started or funded 211 information and referral programs to help people better find the resources.

For you to be sustainable you must figure out what sets you apart from your competition and then build on that advantage. And, frankly, if you do not have an advantage, maybe you need to merge with another nonprofit providing similar services. Ouch! Did I just say, "Merge?" For many nonprofits to even suggest such a thing is horrifying. Yet, the truth is, too many nonprofits are limping along, unable to fully achieve their mission simply because they do not have the competitive advantage.

I urge you to look at all the other similar nonprofits within a 25-mile radius (or further, depending on the geographical range of your services), and do an honest comparison of services. Look at the IRS 990's of your competition (www.irs.gov). Which are the most financially stable? Is it you, or your competition? Which one seems to have the most innovative programs? Which ones are growing, and which ones are not and why?

If you have the competitive advantage do you know why? Are you competing with the other organizations or is there a need for more than one nonprofit to provide similar services? For example, after-school programs often require a proximity to the schools.

In your community are there several nonprofits providing after-school programs? If not, does the need suggest you expand your programs, or should the children be bused from other schools? What makes more sense economically? To bus the children and have the parents drive further to pick them up, or to start satellite programs at each school? If there are other nonprofits providing after-school programs, what geographical area do they cover? Should you be collaborating?

Everything we have talked about up to now in the other seventeen sustainability strategies comes down to this one: competition. Are you good enough to be better than the competition? If you are, then build on that advantage. Expand your marketing. Show why you are better.

But competition is not something we like to talk about within the nonprofit sector. Get over it. We must talk about it. We compete every day for funding, so why not talk about how we are competing for clients if we have the same mission? But should we even be competing? Are there enough clients for all of us? Is there enough funding available for all of us? How do we convince funders that back-to-school programs are just as important, if not more important, than the donation fad of the month?

Answers to these questions are going to vary from one nonprofit to the next. How you answer them will determine whether you have, or should have, the competitive advantage.

Which brings me to the next sustainability strategy: leverage assets through collaboration.

Strategy #19: Leverage Assets through Collaboration

What if, instead of competing with nonprofits providing similar services, we leveraged our assets and worked together? I grit my teeth every time I work on disaster readiness projects within communities. That's because, invariably, local, state and federal government agencies automatically assume they will take the lead when it comes to any disaster. But the reality is the first responders at ANY disaster will be local volunteers. And, if those local volunteers are not prepared or trained, residents lives may be in jeopardy.

It sometimes takes two to three days before government officials can get to disaster areas, especially in remote areas. Local volunteers are usually there immediately. As soon as government agencies show up, they often shove the local people aside and take over. How much better it works for everyone when the government agencies leverage those local assets and collaborate.

In much the same way, local needs are best addressed when all sectors of the community decide to work together. Although we like to think our nonprofit is the best one to address an issue, usually it is more effective when multiple nonprofits work together and collaborate.

Collaboration can be defined as "working together to achieve common goals." Collaboration doesn't necessarily mean giving up anything but can rather mean the sharing of approaches or resources. Let's use the issue of substance abuse among teenagers as an example of the need for collaboration. This issue cuts across multiple sectors: churches, schools, parents, health-care, business, government, and nonprofits. If representatives of these sectors came together and developed a joint plan to address a spike in heroin overdoses, for example, each sector could participate in the education campaign but agree to focus resources on the issue from their unique perspective. None of them gives up any control, but collaborates in their approach toward solving the problem by:

1. Agreeing on a problem statement,
2. Identifying potential solutions,
3. Agreeing to contribute resources,
4. Frequently updating members of the coalition on their efforts.

As each member of the collaboration/coalition works toward reducing the level of heroin overdoses some interesting things happen:
1. There is increased awareness of what each of the partners is doing,
2. There is greater attention focused on the common problem,
3. There are more resources available to solve the problem,
4. The chances of heroin deaths occurring decreases,
5. Gaps in services are identified.

As all the sectors work together and leverage their assets toward a common problem, the chances increase there will be better collaboration in the future on other community issues. It also increases the chances there will be sustainability of the community partners since donors and participants see the value of each partners' mission.

One of the biggest problems in community problem solving is what is sometimes called "the silo effect." (Fig. 10)

This refers to the reality that each of the eight sectors within a community (government, education, health, nonprofits, faith-based, unions, business, citizens) operates within their own silo. In other words, they each have their own language, members/clients, approach, purpose, and bureaucracy.

Thus, collaboration across the sectors is often like dealing with diversity issues. Unless you first address and understand each other's' differences, it will be very difficult to effectively work together.

During one attempt at collaboration at the state level, I was the only representative of the private, non-profit sector. Everyone else in the room was a representative of a state government agency. When the meeting was adjourned, I overheard the chairman of the meeting, who was former military, say to someone, "I just do not understand why Marilyn keeps talking about the role of volunteers. Government is supposed to be in charge." Obviously, he could not get past the silo in his mind to understand the potential role of the nonprofit sector.

The number one roadblock to productive collaboration is ineffective communication, which usually stems from silo-thinking.

Strategy #20: Establish Leadership Role in the Primary Mission

When a nonprofit builds their competitive advantage and then participates in community collaborations, thereby leveraging their assets, they can establish themselves in a leadership role in their specific mission.

But collaboration within community issues is not the only way to establish the nonprofit in a leadership role. When key board members grasp your transformative vision and mission (strategy #2), they can play an important role in advocating for your mission in service clubs and other community organizations. The more knowledgeable and passionate your board members and other key volunteers are, the more likely they are to promote your mission within the community.

If one of your board members is also involved in a local church and someone in the congregation raises questions about child abuse, if your nonprofit is a leader in the issue, he/she will immediately mention your nonprofit. Or, if the local newspaper is doing a story on a family where the parents are arrested for child abuse, will it be your nonprofit they will call for a quote on the topic? If the county commissioners recently did a needs assessment that showed the rates of child abuse have increased due to high rates of unemployment, who will they contact as the frontlines' nonprofit to handle dedicated funding to address the issue? Hopefully it will be you.

Establishing your nonprofit as the leader in the mission of your nonprofit is very important, not just for funding, but for community education and problem-solving. We cannot afford to be so focused on serving our clients that we ignore the needs of the wider community in which we live. Everything we do as a nonprofit sector has a positive impact on our community. Unfortunately, we do not always tout those positive impacts. And we should.

<u>In summary</u>:

Insuring a sustainable nonprofit requires:
1. Building on your competitive advantage,
2. Leveraging your assets through collaboration,
3. Establishing a leadership role based on your primary mission.

Fig. 10 – Community Problem-Solving Sectors or Silos

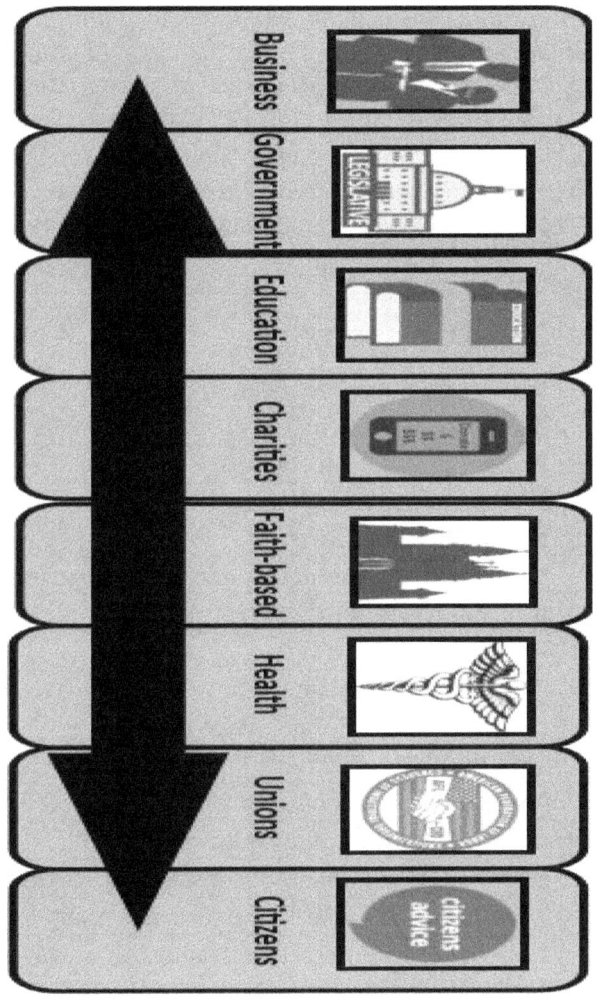

Addendum A: Policies & Procedure Manual Checklist

Indicate with an "x" or a date when the policy/procedure has been finalized in the manual. This should not be regarded as a complete list, but a sample of things to include. Examples of many of the policies and procedures in the checklist are included in the book, "Nonprofit Management Simplified: Internal Operations," ©2017, CharityChannel Press, by M. L. Donnellan, MS, www.amazon.com/author/mldonnellan

X	Category
	Accounting
	Accounts payable procedures
	Billing procedures
	Bank deposit procedures
	Bid and contract policies and procedures
	Budget develop procedures
	Travel expense reimbursement policies, procedures and forms
	Financial management policies and procedures
	Internal management audit checklist
	Board of Directors
	Sample meeting agendas
	Board organizational structure chart
	Officer job descriptions
	Nomination policies and procedures
	Board orientation procedures
	Board member satisfaction surveys, forms
	Legal responsibilities of board members
	Conflict of interest, commitment to serve and confidentiality form

	Board of Directors, cont.
	Board member job description
	Committee job descriptions
	Board member application
	Board demographics matrix (individual and full board)
	Current list of board members and contact information
	Employees
	Hiring packets (I-9, W-4, benefits sign-up forms, employee handbook signature page, payroll deduction forms, etc.)
	Procedures for updating employee handbook
	Procedures and policies related to hiring, firing (job applications, exit interviews, etc.)
	Board-approved jo descriptions for all positions
	Board-approved salary/wage ranges for all positions
	Procedures for updating job descriptions and salary/wage ranges
	Performance review policies and procedures
	ED performance review policies and procedures
	Parking policies and procedures
	Policies and procedures related to the

	building (entrance hours, safety, etc.)
	E-mail
	Policies and procedures for use of email; personal use of company computers
	Equipment
	Vendor files (contracts, maintenance agreement, etc.)
	Inventory policies, procedures, forms

	Files
	Database procedures (updating, security, etc.)
	Mail-merge procedures
	Client files (policies, procedures, confidentiality issues, security, etc.)
	Board member files
	Donor files (policies, procedures, confidentiality, security, etc.)
	Volunteer files (policies, procedures, confidentiality, security, etc.)
	Length of time to keep files
	Accounting files
	Other filing systems
	Internet
	Policies, procedures related to business and personal use of the internet
	Cybersecurity policies, procedures
	Mailings
	Procedures for small and large mailings

	Bulk mailings (when, how, bulk rates)
	Meetings
	Annual meeting sample agenda, minutes, reports
	Board meeting agendas, minutes
	Committee meeting agendas, minutes
	Meeting checklist for room arrangements, food, audio-visuals, etc.
	Office Supplies
	Policies, procedures for ordering supplies
	List of preferred vendors and why
	Publications
	Samples of publications produced by the organization

	Publications, cont.
	Vendor files for printers
	Copyright policies and procedures
	Checklist for approvals of publications
	Strategic Planning
	Policies, procedures, timelines for strategic planning development, implementation and updates; responses to environmental changes
	Timelines
	Organizational timelines (weekly, monthly, annual)
	Volunteers (all types of volunteers: board, committee, program, virtual, volunteers with disabilities)
	Recruitment policies, procedures

	Orientation and training policies, procedures
	Recognition policies, procedures
	Dismissal policies, procedures
	Volunteer handbook(s) development policies and procedures, timelines, updating, etc.

Addendum B: Sample Simplified Strategic Plan

Sample Simplified Strategic Plan
COMMUNITY CHILD ABUSE PREVENTION CENTER

Vision: All children in our community are safe from sexual abuse

Mission: To educate the community, develop effective programs, and support the victims of child abuse

Values: Equal treatment for all...children should be safe....voluntarism is the best way to initiate change, etc.

Slogan: An Open Door to Love

MARKETING and RESOURCE DEVELOPMENT	PROGRAMS and COMMUNITY INVOLVEMENT	ADMINISTRATION and VOLUNTEER DEVELOPMENT
A three year-marketing plan will be developed which will increase brand identity by 30%	A community-wide collaboration of nonprofits addressing similar issues will be convened within one year	A quality management evaluation strategy will be developed and implemented within two years.
A three-year research plan will be developed which will allow for on-going responses by stakeholders and the public to brand awareness strategies	A community-wide needs and resource assessment will be developed, using the collaboration partners as stakeholders.	A plan for increasing the quality and quantity of facility space will be developed within the next year.
Within one year all material used by the nonprofit will reflect brand identity strategies and logo.	The nonprofit will be a catalyst for the development of a community-wide plan for reducing the number of child abuse victims.	A system of internal financial controls will be developed and implemented for testing by board members within one year.
A three-year fundraising plan will be developed which will increase financial resources by 30% per year.	Each program will develop 3-5 year plans for implementation of outcome measurement strategies within one year	A board-level committee will research and develop suitable risk management policies and strategies.
The number of grants written will increase 25% per year.	Each program will develop case statements to be used by marketing and will update them annually, based on outcomes measurements results	A detailed policies and procedures manual will be developed within two years
A planned giving program will be established, with the first $100,000 bequest within two years.	Each program will be responsible for the development of annual budgets to be given to the ED at least one month before the annual organizational budget is due	A Volunteer Development Committee will be established to develop recruitment, training, recognition and dismissal policies and procedures for all types of volunteers
On-going research will identify at least one new potential fundraising market per year.	Long-term sustainability strategies will be developed for each program within one year	A hyperlinked, on-line volunteer handbook will be developed and be available for all volunteers within one year
Internal and external case statements will be developed and updated annually, to be used for all marketing and resource development strategies	Staff succession plans will be developed for each program	A virtual volunteer plan will be implemented within two years.
Annual RD evaluations will show no more than 20% of funding comes from any one source	Annual program evaluations will demonstrate by research-based outcomes measurements the validity of the programs	Senior staff and key volunteer succession plans will be developed within one year
Annual evaluations will show expenses on all RD strategies are less than 30%	Each program will contribute client videos demonstrating successes of outcomes	A technology and software 5-year plan will be developed, including budget, within one year

Addendum C: Sample Committee Chair & Vice Chair Job Descriptions

Title: Committee Chairperson

Reports to, selected and evaluated by:
Board of Directors

Term: One year, from election at the annual meeting until the next annual meeting.

Attendance requirements: As a member of the Board of Directors, the Committee Chair adheres to the same attendance requirements as a board member, with additional attendance at the Executive Committee meetings.

Responsibilities:

- Meeting facilitation – Serves as the facilitator of the Committee meetings; may be asked to facilitate the Executive Committee or Board meetings in the absence of the Chair
- Staff Advisory – Acts as advisor to the Committee staff between board meetings on relevant matters
- Board advisory – Assures that the Committee provides advice to the board in the designated area of responsibility for the committee, developing policies to present to the board as needed.

(From the bylaws, Article V, Sec. 6) "In the absence of the Chair of the Board or in the event of his/her inability or refusal to act, a Vice-chair shall be appointed to perform the duties of Chair of the Board, and when so acting, shall have all the powers of and be subject to all the restrictions upon the Chair of the Board. Committee Chairs of the Board shall serve as Vice-chair s of the Board. The Committee Chairs of the Board shall perform such other duties as from time to time may be assigned to them by the chair of the Board or by the Board of Directors."

Commitment:

- To facilitate all meetings in a neutral manner, encouraging input and participation by everyone in attendance
- To provide leadership to the Committee and assure adherence to the policies, ethics, values, vision and mission of the organization when developing recommendations for the Board or staff
- To provide appropriate evaluation and recognition of staff and volunteer efforts within the Committee.

Time Commitment:

In addition to the board member time commitment, approximately four hours per quarter for advisory duties to staff, facilitation of committee meeting, and attendance at Executive Committee meetings, and monitoring of volunteer efforts related to the designated Committee.

Title: Vice-Chair of Committee
Reports to, selected and evaluated by: Board of Directors
Term: One year, from election at the annual meeting until the next annual meeting.
Attendance requirements: As a member of the Board of Directors, the Committee Vice-Chair adheres to the same attendance requirements as a board member, with additional attendance at the Executive Committee meetings.
Responsibilities:
- Meeting facilitation – Serves as the facilitator of the Committee meetings in the absence of the Committee Chair; may be asked to facilitate the Executive Committee or Board meetings in the absence of the Board Chair or Committee Chair
- Leadership Development – To assimilate historical, policy and procedural information with a goal toward potential additional leadership within the organization.

(From the bylaws, Article V, Sec. 1) "The Officers of the Corporation shall be a Chair of the Board, Committee Chairs, Committee Vice-Chairs…."; Article V, Sec. 6: "In the absence of the Chair of the Board or in the event of his/her inability or refusal to act, a Vice-chair shall be appointed to perform the duties of Chair of the Board, and when so acting, shall have all the powers of and be subject to all the restrictions upon the Chair of the Board. Committee Vice-Chairs of the Board shall serve as Vice-Chairs of the Committees of the Corporation. The Committee Vice-Chairs of the Board shall perform such other duties as from time to time may be assigned to them by the chair of the Board, the Committee Chair, or by the Board of Directors."

Commitment:

1. When asked, to facilitate all meetings in a neutral manner, encouraging input and participation by everyone in attendance
2. To observe the leadership to the Committee and assure adherence to the policies, ethics, values, vision and mission of the organization when developing recommendations for the Board or staff
3. To support the Committee Chair as needed
4. To assume the leadership of the committee when the Committee Chair's term is up if so requested by the Nominating

Committee.

Time Commitment:

In addition to the board member time commitment, approximately three hours per quarter as needed for attendance at Executive Committee meeting and interaction with the Committee Chair and designated staff.

Addendum D: Sample Officer Job Descriptions

Title: Chair of the Board
Reports to, selected and evaluated by: Board of Directors
Term: One year, with an additional year as Past Chair of the Board, beginning with the election at the annual meeting and ending the next annual meeting.
Attendance Requirements: As a member of the Board of Directors, the Chair adheres to the same attendance requirements as a board member, with additional attendance at the Executive Committee meetings. The Chair also serves as a voting, ex-officio member of all committees and task forces.
Responsibilities:
- Meeting facilitation – Serves as the facilitator of all board meetings and Executive Committee meetings, with voting privileges only in the event of a tie vote
- Spokesperson – Along with the ED, serves as the official spokesperson for the organization in all matters
- Supervisor – Serves as the supervisor of the ED.

(From the bylaws, Article V, Sec. 5: "The Chair of the Board shall be the principal officer of the Corporation. He/She shall preside at all meetings of the members and of the Board of Directors. He/She may sign, with the Secretary or any other proper Officer of the Corporation authorized by the Board of Directors, any deeds, mortgages, contracts or other instruments which the Board of Directors has authorized to be executed, except in cases where the signing and execution thereof shall be expressly delegated by the Board of Directors or by these Bylaws or be granted by statute to some other Officer or agent of the Corporation; and, in general, he/she shall perform all duties incident to the office of Chair of the Board and such other duties as may be prescribed by the Board of Directors from time to time.

He/She shall be voting, ex-officio member of all management divisions and board-appointed committees.")

Commitment:
- To facilitate all meetings in a neutral manner, encouraging input and participation by everyone in attendance
- To provide leadership to the organization to assure adherence to the policies, ethics, values, vision and mission of the organization
- To understand and monitor all legal aspects of the organization
- To seek ways to promote the organization in the community, in the state and nationally, and to convey to the board local, state and national issues which have the potential to impact the organization

- To assure appropriate evaluation and recognition of staff and volunteer efforts
- To serve as past chair of the board upon the completion of the term of office as Chair, upon the request of the Nominating Committee

Time Commitment:
In addition to the board member and Executive Committee time commitment, approximately one hour per week for organizational duties and for monitoring staff and volunteer efforts.

Title: Treasurer
Reports to, selected and evaluated by: Board of Directors

Term: One year, from election at the annual meeting until the next annual meeting.

Attendance requirements: As a member of the Board of Directors, the Treasurer adheres to the same attendance requirements as a board member, with additional attendance at the Executive Committee meetings.

Responsibilities:
(Per Article V, Sec. 7 "The Treasurer shall have charge and custody of, be responsible for, and shall cause to be administered all funds and securities of the Corporation; receive and give receipts for monies due and payable to the Corporation from any source whatsoever,

deposit all such monies in the name of the Corporation in such banks, trust companies or other depositories as shall be selected in accordance with the provisions of Article XI, Sec. 3 of these Bylaws; and in general, perform all the duties incident to the office of Treasurer and such other duties as from time to time may be assigned to him/her by the Chair of the Board or by the Board of Directors."

Commitment:

To assure implementation of all financial management policies and procedures in accordance with the Standards of Accounting for Nonprofits and all legal requirements related to finances;

To serve as a member of the Administration/Internal Operations, and Executive Committees; To consider serving as vice-chair of the board, then board chair and past chair of the board, depending on the recommendations of the nominating committee.

Time Commitment:

In addition to the board member and Executive Committee time commitment, approximately one hour per week for duties associated with the office.

Addendum E: Simplified Parliamentary Procedure

Kind of Motion	Object of Motion	Effect of Motion
"Table"	Clear the floor for more urgent business	Delays action
"Question"	Secure immediate vote on pending motion; must be called by a member of the group, not the chair	Ends debate
"Limit/extend time"	Provides more/less time for discussion	Shortens/lengthens time for debate discussion period
"Postpone definitely" (to a certain time)	Gives more time for informal discussion and for securing followers/support	Delays action
"Commit/refer" (to committee)	Enables more careful consideration to be given before a vote; allows for more information to be gathered before a vote	Delays action
"Amend"	Improve the motion	Change the original motion
"Postpone indefinitely"	Prevents a vote on the question (motion)	Suppress the question (motion)
"Point of order"	Call attention to violation of	Maintains parliamentary

	parliamentary procedure	procedures
"Appeal the decision of the chair"	To determine the group's attitude on the ruling by the chair	Secures ruling by group, rather than by the chair
"Move"	To bring an item to a vote	Stops discussion temporarily; requires second for action by group
"Second"	Moves motion to action	Forces group to take specific action
"Discussion"	Discussion on motion	Gives chance for additional discussion on seconded motion
"Say 'aye or nay'"	Calls for the vote (Generally, the chair does not vote, unless needed to break a tie, and only members of the group can vote)	Ends discussion and asks for group consensus

Addendum F: Sustainability Assessment

Score your nonprofit in each of the 20 strategies. At the end of the chart is a total ratings chart. Use the following scores:
0=Never
1=Rarely
2=Once in a while
3=Sometimes
4=Frequently
5=Always

Sustainability Strategy	Score
#1 – Balance the core elements in the infrastructure	
#2 – Establish clear and transformative vision and mission statements	
#3 – Embed metrics across the organization	
#4 – Implement a never-ending strategic planning process	
#5 – Establish an outcomes measurements process for every facet of the organization	
#6 – Build relevant programs	
#7 – Diversify funding sources	
#8 – Annually evaluate fundraising costs vs. income for every strategy used	
#9 – Implement a senior staff succession plan	
#10 – Establish institutional memory collection procedures	

#11 – Implement accelerating technologies strategies	
#12 – Outsource when appropriate	
#13 – Implement a key-volunteer succession plan	
#14 – Establish regular board training	
#15 – Recruit high capacity volunteers	
#16 – Integrate marketing through the nonprofit	
#17 – Demonstrate value to the community	
#18 – Build on competitive advantage in the community	
#19 – Leverage assets thru collaboration	
#20 – Establish leadership role in the community, based on the primary mission	

Total all columns and then add them and see how the grand total compares to the following chart:

Grand Total	Sustainability
85-100	Very sustainable
60-84	Somewhat sustainable
35-59	Not very sustainable
1-34	Not at all sustainable

This is not a scientific assessment but is meant to provide you with some guidance in determining if your nonprofit is sustainable.

About the Author

Marilyn L. Donnellan, MS has more than 35 years' experience as a non-profit CEO and consultant. The non-profits where she served ranged in size from a single staff organization with a budget of $150,000 to a $6 million non-profit with 300 staff. She is the author of numerous articles in nonprofit trade journals and her books on nonprofit management are in use in more than a dozen countries. She has a B.A. degree in Human Resources Management from George Fox University and an M.S. degree in Administration from Atlantic Coast Theological Seminary.

Other Books by Donnellan

The Complete Guide to Church Management (English), Xulon Press,
www.amazon.com/author/mldonnellan
The Complete Guide to Church Management (Chichewa), *www.mldonnellan.com*
Nonprofit Management Simplified: Internal Operations, ©2017, CharityChannel Press,
www.amazon.com/author/mldonnellan
Nonprofit Management Simplified: Board and Volunteer Development, ©2017, CharityChannel Press,
www.amazon.com/author/mldonnellan

Nonprofit Management Simplified: Programs and Fundraising, ©2017, CharityChannel Press, *www.amazon.com/author/mldonnellan*
Two Faces of Me, *www.amazon.com/author/mldonnellan*
Give 'til it Hurts (fiction)
http://smashwords.com/books/view/772465

Connect with the Author

mldonnellanauthor@gmail.com
www.mldonnellan.com

www.ingramcontent.com/pod-product-compliance
Lightning Source LLC
Chambersburg PA
CBHW070154230526
45471CB00002B/653